YOUR
Camels
Are
Coming

Inkwell Heritage Publishing

18896 Greenwell Springs Road
Greenwell Springs, LA 70739

YOUR
Camels
Are
Coming

THE BRIDE'S JOURNEY
TO DESTINY

by

Andrea "Andy" McDougal

Published by:

Inkwell Heritage Publishing
18896 Greenwell Springs Road
Greenwell Springs, LA 70739

ISBN 989-8-9987460-2-4

Printed on demand in the US, the UK and Australia
For Worldwide Distribution

Dedication

I dedicate this book to the One who saved me, the One who has kept me, the One who owns me and purchased me with a great price — my Adonai!

He is the Lover of my soul. He is the Giver of life. He is Knowledge, He is my Joy and my Comforter. He is Revelation and the One who unlocks the key to His Word!

I thank Him for the many times He visited me when I was a child and a teen, giving me glimpses of my destiny.

Acknowledgments

I must acknowledge the contribution of my editors. Even though I have taught these words over the years and I am the author of this book, I could never have put it together without their help. Thank you.

Other Books by
Andrea McDougal

The Glory of God Revealed

His Wonders in the Deep

The Power of the Seed

The Arrows of the Lord

A Southern Lady's Tea Journey

A Southern Lady's Tea Adventures

Contents

Genesis 24:1-27

¹ *Now Abraham was old, well advanced in years, and the Lord had blessed Abraham in all things.* ² *And Abraham said to the eldest servant of his house [Eliezer of Damascus], who ruled over all that he had, I beg of you, put your hand under my thigh;* ³ *and you shall swear by the Lord, the God of heaven and earth, that you will not take a wife for my son from the daughters of the Canaanites, among whom I have settled,* ⁴ *but you shall go to my country and to my relatives and take a wife for my son Isaac.*

⁵ *The servant said to him, But perhaps the woman will not be willing to come along after me to this country. Must I take your son to the country from which you came?*

⁶ *Abraham said to him, See to it that you do not take my son back there.* ⁷ *The Lord, the God of heaven, Who took me from my father's house, from the land of my family and my birth, Who spoke to me and swore to me, saying, To your offspring I will give this land — He will send His Angel before you, and you will take a wife from there for my son.* ⁸ *And if the woman should not be willing to go along after you, then you will be clear from this oath; only you must not take my son back there.*

⁹ *So the servant put his hand under the thigh of Abra-*

ham his master and swore to him concerning this matter. ¹⁰ And the servant took ten of his master's camels and departed, taking some of all his master's treasures with him; thus he journeyed to Mesopotamia [between the Tigris and the Euphrates], to the city of Nahor [Abraham's brother]. ¹¹ And he made his camels to kneel down outside the city by a well of water at the time of the evening when women go out to draw water.

¹² And he said, O Lord, God of my master Abraham, I pray You, cause me to meet with good success today, and show kindness to my master Abraham. ¹³ See, I stand here by the well of water, and the daughters of the men of the city are coming to draw water. ¹⁴ And let it so be that the girl to whom I say, I pray you, let down your jar that I may drink, and she replies, Drink, and I will give your camels drink also — let her be the one whom You have selected and appointed and indicated for Your servant Isaac [to be a wife to him]; and by it I shall know that You have shown kindness and faithfulness to my master.

¹⁵ Before he had finished speaking, behold, out came Rebekah, who was the daughter of Bethuel son of Milcah, who was the wife of Nahor the brother of Abraham, with her water jar on her shoulder. ¹⁶ And the girl was very beautiful and attractive, chaste and modest, and unmarried. And she went down to the well, filled her water jar, and came up.

¹⁷ And the servant ran to meet her, and said, I pray you, let me drink a little water from your water jar.

¹⁸ And she said, Drink, my lord; and she quickly let down her jar onto her hand and gave him a drink.

¹⁹ When she had given him a drink, she said, I will draw water for your camels also, until they finish drinking. ²⁰ So she quickly emptied her jar into the trough and ran again to the well and drew water for all his camels. ²¹ The man stood gazing at her in silence, waiting to know if the Lord had made his trip prosperous.

²² And when the camels had finished drinking, the man took a gold earring or nose ring of half a shekel in weight, and for her hands two bracelets of ten shekels in weight in gold, ²³ and said, Whose daughter are you? I pray you, tell me: Is there room in your father's house for us to lodge there?

²⁴ And she said to him, I am the daughter of Bethuel son of Milcah and [her husband] Nahor.

²⁵ She said also to him, We have both straw and provender (fodder) enough, and also room in which to lodge.

²⁶ The man bowed down his head and worshiped the Lord ²⁷ and said, Blessed be the Lord, the God of my master Abraham, Who has not left my master bereft and destitute of His loving-kindness and steadfastness. As for me, going on the way [of obedience and faith] the Lord led me to the house of my master's kinsmen.

Introduction

In the beautiful Old Testament story of Abraham's search for a suitable bride for his son Isaac, the patriarch Abraham is a type of God, the Father; Isaac is a type of Christ, our Redeemer; Eliezer, Abraham's faithful servant, is a type of the Holy Spirit; and Rebekah is a type of the Third-Day Bride of Christ, who will be found worthy to unite with Him for all eternity. It was Eliezer who was chosen and sent by Abraham to a distant land to seek the needed bride, and as he departed with ten heavily-laden camels, the Scriptures state: *"All the goods of his master were in his hand"* (Genesis 24:10, KJV). WOW!

What was the reason Eliezer loaded those camels so heavily? Yes, he would need provisions for the journey, going and coming, but most of the goods loaded on the backs of the camels that day were not for Eliezer or his men. Rather, they were intended as gifts for the prospective bride.

Abraham was a very wealthy man, and the gifts he sent must represent that wealth and the type of life he was inviting some worthy woman to share with the one who was soon to be heir of his vast fortune.

For many days those heavily-loaded camels were en route to the city of Nahor, where Eliezer would happen upon a young woman named Rebekah, whom he would find drawing water at the town well. What day it would actually happen she could not have known; nor could she have known for certain that it would happen. She just had to be ready for whatever came her way. Rebekah's day of destiny was approaching on the backs of those camels, but she could not have known that. Had she somehow sensed that the moment of her fulfillment was upon her? Or, like most of us, were the trials of daily life getting the best of her at the moment?

If all went as planned, before long the pouches on those camels' backs would be opened, and rare gifts would be lavished upon her. Would she be ready for that moment? Or would something else distract her? Would she perhaps refuse to embrace

WHAT DAY IT WOULD
ACTUALLY HAPPEN
SHE COULD NOT HAVE
KNOWN; NOR COULD
SHE HAVE KNOWN
FOR CERTAIN THAT IT
WOULD HAPPEN. SHE
JUST HAD TO BE READY
FOR WHATEVER CAME
HER WAY!

the smelly animals that unknowingly bore her future on their backs? The Scriptures warn us not to miss the "day" or "time" of our "visitation," and what might cause you to miss the day of your visitation?

If Rebekah could only overcome the distractions of the day — perhaps the petty jealousies of other young women, the whisperings and snickerings of the elderly, or the lurid suggestions of the carnal men who may have frequented the area looking for easy prey — those gifts would be hers. And that was to be just the beginning. These were just preliminary gifts. Many more would later be offered, for both her and her family.

And still the best was yet to come. When Rebekah eventually became Isaac's bride, all that he had would become hers. In the same way, when we became the Bride of Christ, through our covenant with Him, everything that is His becomes ours.

But first Rebekah would have to choose to make the journey to meet her beloved. It was a day of momentous decision, for her camels were coming.

And what does all this mean to you today? I want to tell you that *your* camels are also on their way. What God has destined for you, as part of the Bride of Christ, is even now on its way to you, and it will eventually reach you — if you haven't grown discouraged and given up while waiting. You can't afford to do that, for *YOUR Camels Are Coming!*

Andrea "Andy" McDougal
Baton Rouge, Louisiana

CHAPTER 1

The Pros and Cons of Camels

And the servant took ten camels of the camels of his master, and departed; for all the goods of his master were in his hand: and he arose, and went.
Genesis 24:10, KJV

Camels ... you either love them or hate them. They have many interesting attributes, some of which are good and some of which are bad. Here, first, are some of the good ones.

The Positive Attributes of Camels

Camels are sure-footed in rocky terrain, on soft and shifting sandy soil, and in mountainous ar-

21

eas. They are especially suited to the deserts, for the pads on their feet spread in a way that keeps them from sinking into soft sand. They can travel places where horses and mules cannot go. Camels are also strong swimmers and can easily cross great rivers.

Camels are most famous for their ability to go without water for many days. They thrive in very hot, dry climates, such as deserts or a wilderness. (*Webster's* has defined a *wilderness* as "a beautiful garden that is void of the Master's hand.")

A camel's eyes are not like that of a man. When a sandstorm is upon a caravan, the camels are able to continue seeing in the midst of the storm, even when no other animal or man can. Thus, a camel will continue on a difficult journey, when no man or other beast would be able to. A camel can survive the harshest of elements where other creatures would perish.

Camels, it seems, are ideally suited for carrying very heavy loads through the scorching heat of desert places. In the Spirit, God's camels leave the heavenlies and travel through the deserts of our lives to reach us with His provisions. They are very sure-footed, as they travel through the wildernesses of our lives, and always arrive at the appropriate time.

IN THE SPIRIT, GOD'S CAMELS LEAVE THE HEAVENLIES AND TRAVEL THROUGH THE DESERTS OF OUR LIVES TO REACH US WITH HIS PROVISIONS. THEY ARE VERY SURE-FOOTED AND ALWAYS ARRIVE AT THE APPROPRIATE TIME!

In the natural, it is evident that camels were created by God for a very specific and useful purpose. In the Spirit, He sends them to us in our time of need.

In the natural, there is nothing much appealing or beautiful about a camel, but when you see them traveling through harsh territories, and they are fulfilling their divinely-ordered purpose, they suddenly become magnificent, beautiful and glorious creatures, and we need more of them in our lives.

The Negative Attributes of Camels

Then there are the negative aspects of camels. Camels are ugly, smelly, obnoxious, stubborn, obstinate, unreasonable, awkward and noisy beasts, and that turns a lot of people off.

Yes, camels are notoriously ugly. When you look at one of them up close, there is absolutely nothing appealing about them. They are not glorified-looking animals in any sense of the word. Horses are beautiful, but camels are just plain ugly.

Yes, camels are notoriously smelly. They stink, and part of their obnoxious odor is due to the fact that they are cud-chewing animals, ruminators. If they don't like what you're trying to make them do, they will regurgitate a very foul-smelling substance and spit it on you or around you. No one likes that.

Yes, camels are notoriously stubborn. They have a mind of their own, and they're very strong willed. If they don't get what they want when they want it, they tend to bite the person nearest to them and make life generally miserable for everyone.

Yes, camels are notoriously unreasonable. There is absolutely no reasoning with them. You cannot talk them into your way of thinking. You cannot reason with them at all. And you also cannot make them leave you alone if they don't want to. If they are set on staying with you, nothing can change their minds,

Yes, camels are notoriously awkward and very difficult to ride. To do it successfully, you have to learn to flow with their movements. They move with their two right legs at the same time and then with their two left legs at the same time. Because of this, they rock back and forth from one side to the other. Because they rock much like a boat does, someone attempting to ride a camel can easily become seasick.

Yes, camels are notoriously noisy. They snort a lot and make other loud and obnoxious sounds.

WE DON'T REALLY SEE
CAMELS COMING TO
OUR DOOR IN THIS DAY
AND AGE, BUT THERE ARE
SITUATIONS AND PEOPLE
IN OUR LIVES THAT WE
ARE NOT SURE HOW TO
DEAL WITH!

Even while you're trying to communicate with them, they keep on snorting.

The Camels in Your Life

There may be some camels already evident in your life, and you haven't known what to do with them. Some ugly, stinking creatures may have come to your front door, and you weren't sure if you should invite them in or drive them away. Be careful, for they may be the camels which are bringing God's favor upon your life.

Of course, this is spiritually speaking. We don't really see camels coming to our door in this day and age, but there are situations and people in our lives that we are not sure how to deal with.

When you see your camels approaching, your first thought may be, "No! No! This cannot be God!" You may have actually run from such animals. You may have tried to cast them out or drive them away. You may have commanded them to leave in the name of Jesus. But isn't it true that God comes to us in the most unusual ways and under the most unusual circumstances, to bring us His blessings?

You may have thought that your more recent days have been the worst in your lifetime, but that may be because your camels have arrived, and you just didn't realize their importance and have been rebuking them. What you have been experiencing may mean that you are about to receive a blessing. The Lord is allowing something to come into your life that will bring you closer to your destiny.

As we are about to see, the coming of the camels to Rebekah was a test for her. She was about to be blessed, but could she accept the means God had chosen to deliver her blessing? Her gifts were ready, but they were hidden on the backs of some frightful-looking beasts.

On one of my trips to Israel, I was encouraged to ride a camel. It was the dirtiest, nastiest animal I'd ever seen. He had little prickly hairs sticking out all over his face, and I thought he was the ugliest creature I'd ever laid eyes on. I didn't want anything to do with him.

On another day, I saw a camel sitting down outside the gates of the Old City of Jerusalem. This one was very different. He was so clean and so beautifully arrayed that tourists immediately wanted to get on him and have their pictures taken. This camel was very appealing. This should teach us all a lesson. Sometimes the things that we reject out of hand and think are surely from the devil and need to be rebuked and sent on their way are the very things God will use to bring us His blessing.

Be more careful how you handle the situations and the people you come in contact with in life. Get ready, for *YOUR Camels Are Coming!*

CHAPTER 2

"At Sundry Times and in Divers Manners"

God, who at sundry times and in divers man-
ners spake in time past unto the fathers by the
prophets, hath in these last days spoken unto us
by his Son, whom he hath appointed heir of all
things, by whom also he made the worlds.

Hebrews 1:1-2, KJV

Before we get to the story of Abraham's camels and their meaning to us today, let's stop and think about how God reveals His wonderful mysteries to us.

Many Bible scholars believe that Paul was the writer of the letter to the Hebrews, while others disagree. Since the book does not bear the writer's name, we cannot know for sure. But that's not the important point we need to glean from this powerful opening statement to this particular book of the Bible. The important thing to note is that, in this awesome way, the writer to the Hebrews (whoever he was) chose to emphasize the manner in which God brought forth to the world the greatest revelation of all times.

Not Just Any News

This was not just any news that God was revealing. It was the revelation of the Christ, the Anointed One, the only true and living God, the only One who could purge us of our sins, and the One who has now resumed His place at the right hand of the Father in Heaven. Christ's coming to earth was to be the answer to every need of mankind throughout the ages, and no revelation has ever been more important. Therefore it is also important to note the way in which God chose to reveal this great truth.

The Method of Revelation

The writer of the Hebrews says that *"God ... spoke,"* and, for certain, that was nothing new. What is so important to us today is the way in which He spoke.

THE IMPORTANT THING
TO NOTE IS THAT, IN
THIS AWESOME WAY, THE
WRITER TO THE HEBREWS
CHOSE TO EMPHASIZE
THE MANNER IN WHICH
GOD BROUGHT FORTH
TO THE WORLD THE
GREATEST REVELATION
OF ALL TIMES!

Not surprisingly, the writer also emphasizes that God spoke forth this revelation *"by the prophets."* This was also not unexpected, and we can easily understand God's reasons for doing it this way. Again, what seems to be surprising to many of us is the *way* in which God chose to use these prophets to reveal this great truth.

The Amplified Bible (one of my personal favorites) renders this first verse of Hebrews in the following way:

> *In many separate revelations, [each of which set forth a portion of the Truth] and in different ways God spoke of old to [our] forefathers in and by the prophets.*

What is the writer saying? He is saying that God didn't give this most important revelation ever shown to mankind all at once. He chose to give it to us *"in many separate revelations,"* and each of those revelations only *"set forth a portion of the Truth."* Now, when you stop to think about it, this is remarkable for many reasons.

Often Skipped Over

These opening words of Hebrews have often been skipped over, as if they had little meaning at all. In reality, they are full of meaning, and that meaning was not just for the people of the first century. It is also for you and me today in the twenty-first century.

What is the writer saying that was (and still is) so important? He was saying that God moved; He spoke; He revealed; He released a revelation; He provided some vital information; and nothing could have been more important.

What was being addressed in God's words of revelation through the various prophets was literally a matter of life and death for every man, woman, boy and girl alive on the face of the earth at any given time. But it was even more important than life and death; it actually meant the difference between eternal life and eternal death. What God was saying held the keys to the complete redemption of the world and of each individual in that world.

If you had a message that could save the lives of millions of people, how would you deliver it? Surprisingly, God chose to deliver such a message in bits and pieces, through a variety of vessels, in a

THE REVELATION DID COME, THE PROVISION WAS MADE, AND THE GOOD NEWS WAS SPREAD, BUT IT WAS DONE IN GOD'S TIME AND IN HIS WAY — PIECE BY PIECE, *"AT SUNDRY TIMES AND IN DIVERS MANNERS!"*

variety of places, at various times and under various circumstances. That surely would not be our method, and yet God chose this strange means to deliver His message.

What Was God's Message?

What was God's message to mankind? It was that He had the answer for the ills that daily threatened the welfare and happiness of men and women everywhere, and if they would only turn to Him, they would be saved. And yet He did not give this revelation all at once or in a short space of time or even in one place. Instead, He chose to deliver it piece by piece, through a variety of servants, in a variety of places and under a variety of circumstances.

The revelation did come, the provision was made, and the Good News was spread, but it was done in God's time and in His way — piece by piece, *"at sundry times and in divers manners."*

It was never God's intention to withhold anything from His children. He was ready to give all that was needed. His Word is clear on the fact that He will never withhold His goodness from those who are His. And yet there was a very specific timing involved with it all, and God controlled the clock.

Why?

Why would the writer begin his letter with such words? Because this is God's way, and that's just as true today as it was when our forefathers were seeking Him. If we can learn God's way, we will save ourselves many heartaches and many sorrows. So, let's look at these words more closely.

> *God, who at sundry times and in divers manners spake in time past unto the fathers by the prophets, hath in these last days spoken unto us by his Son, whom he hath appointed heir of all things, by whom also he made the worlds.*
>
> Hebrews 1:1-2, KJV

This word *sundry* is translated from the Greek word *polumeros,* and according to *Strong's* (#4181) conveys the meaning *"in many portions, i.e. variously as to time and agency (piecemeal)."*

Strong's (#3313) further defines the word as meaning *"various, miscellaneous ways, devices, separate, individual ways, in many parts and ways."*

Webster's Dictionary defines *sundry* in the following way: *"piecemeal, a small bit, a fragment, made or done in single, separate parts and pieces, piece by piece, in small amounts or degrees."* All of this should help

IF WE CAN LEARN GOD'S WAY, WE WILL SAVE OURSELVES MANY HEARTACHES AND MANY SORROWS!

us to understand better how God chose to reveal
Jesus to the world.

Is It Still Important?

But since we already have the revelation of Jesus
Christ today, is all of this still important to us? I
believe it is very important, and the reason is that
God hasn't changed. This is still His way of doing
things. He doesn't dump the total revelation on
you all at once. You couldn't handle it. He doesn't
change you all at once. You would be ripped apart.
He doesn't give you all of His power at once. You
couldn't bear it. You would explode.

God is still at work in the world, He is still speaking through His prophets, and He is still bringing
about the fulfillment of all that He promised, but
He does it in this same deliberate and determined
way, piece by piece, here a little and there a little,
over a period of time, through a variety of vessels,
and in a variety of circumstances.

So what can you do? Eagerly receive each piece
of the puzzle revealed to you, guard it with your
life and then excitedly wait for the next piece, until
at last you will have the whole. Just as Jesus was
surely coming to the world, YOUR blessing is just
as sure to come.

Are These Archaic Words?

Does the word *sundry* mean anything to us today? Was this just some archaic vocabulary word used by the ancients? Is this just another out-of-date King James word that fails to relate to our modern world? No, not at all. *Sundry* can become a very exciting word for those who will pause long enough to grasp its promise.

The writer to the Hebrews, just as the other writers whom God used to form the body of anointed literature we now know as His Holy Word, was a man in touch with the Almighty, a man who not only knew God, but who also understood God's ways. It was because of this that he chose to preface the rest of his writings with this mysterious statement about how God did things in the past.

Thank God for these words because they reveal to us how God is still doing things and how He will do things in the future. His blessings will come to you *"at sundry times and in divers ways,"* not all in one great indigestible chunk. But they will surely come.

The revelation of Jesus Christ and the understanding of that revelation came over a period of many years, it came through many different prophets and patriarchs, and it came through

HE IS STILL JEHOVAH JIREH, THE ONE WHO SEES YOUR SITUATION AND RUNS OUT AHEAD OF YOU TO TAKE CARE OF IT!

many shadows and types. And our God, who is *"the same, yesterday, today … and forever"* (Hebrews 13:8), is still revealing Himself in this same way.

Does the fact that God reveals Himself in degrees and over time suggest, in any way, that He has stopped fulfilling His promises or that He no longer does miracles? No! Quite the contrary! God is never slow to move. He is still Jehovah Jireh, the One who sees your situation and runs out ahead of you to take care of it.

Things Held in Reserve

I've always believed that there are things held in reserve for each of us, and they will be released at the appropriate time. This might include a healing, a financial blessing, a revelation or a ministry. When that appropriate time comes (and only God knows when that is), the needed favor will be released. You can count on it.

This is not a time for discouragement; it's a very exciting time. God still moves and He still speaks. The fact that He does it *"at sundry times and in diverse manners"* should not discourage anyone. That's the only way we could handle His blessings.

God has not given up on this world as a whole, and He has not given up on you as an individual.

He is still interested in this world, and He is still interested in its individual parts. And that means YOU. It is still the Father's good pleasure to give to YOU the Kingdom (see Luke 12:32) and to provide YOU the abundant life He so powerfully promised in John 10:10.

This is a book about faith, a book that should cause hope and faith to be stirred in your heart. But it must go far beyond the stirring. I'm believing for faith to be released in your life so that the things which are not yet tangible become so to you today and in the days ahead.

Your promise *will* be fulfilled. You may not have seen it yet, but it's on its way. All that you need, all that is required for an abundant life is even now making its way to you. *YOUR Camels Are Coming!*

"Here a Little and There a Little"

For precept must be upon precept, precept upon precept; line upon line, line upon line; here a little, and there a little. Isaiah 28:9, KJV

For it is [His prophets repeating over and over]: precept upon precept, precept upon precept, rule upon rule, rule upon rule; here a little, there a little. AMP

This is the way in which God does things, not all at once, and not everything in one big shot, but rather little by little, *"precept upon precept," "line upon line," "here a little and there a little."*

We Often Don't Like It

We don't much like the fact that God works in this way because we want it all NOW, but our God is wiser than men, and He knows what we can handle at any given time. Because of His love for us and His desire for our very best, He will always do things in His own way and in His own time — never in ours. Father always knows best.

This matter of timing has been, at times, a point of personal confusion for me. Many times, when I was ministering to others, I saw instant miracles. People came to our meetings with severe needs, we prayed, and those prayers were immediately answered. Sick came and were instantly healed. People came with bad backs and were instantly healed. People even came with broken bones, and they, too, were instantly healed.

Some cases were extremely urgent. An eighteen-year-old girl who was going blind attended our meetings. She had been diagnosed with severe glaucoma. When I prayed for her, God's power hit her in a way she had never experienced before. It came upon her so strongly that she was thrown backward into a chair. The result was that she was instantly healed. She went back to her doctor and came again bearing the medical reports of her

WE WANT IT ALL NOW, BUT OUR GOD IS WISER THAN MEN, AND HE KNOWS WHAT WE CAN HANDLE AT ANY GIVEN TIME!

condition before and after prayer. Her healing had been confirmed.

In this same way, many miraculous things happened instantaneously as we prayed. But, even though I had faith to believe for instant miracles for others, when it came to my own needs, it seemed that I did not receive the same instant miracles that were happening over and over with those I prayed for. Again and again, I had to wait on God for my own miracles, and that was the hardest thing to do, especially after I had seen so many others get instantaneous answers.

It Didn't Make Sense

In many ways, that didn't make sense to me ... until I began to understand the timings of God. I can't tell you how many times I prayed, "God, I've seen You do so many mighty things, and yet it seems like it's taking forever for my own healing to come." It was through pondering this apparent contradiction in faith that I began to understand Him more fully. I knew that He was Jehovah Jireh and that He not only provides our needs, but He knows them in advance and runs out ahead of us to deal with them. So what was I doing wrong? Why was I able to get answers for others and yet could not seem to get answers for myself?

When comprehension finally came to me, it was powerful. I began to think: How long had those people who came to my meetings been believing for their healing? How long had they been believing for their breakthrough? How many times had they prayed? I was blessed to be there at the moment God chose to give them their miracle, and so it always seemed instantaneous to me. But it could not have been the same for them. They'd had to wait for that appointed time and that appointed place. The deliverance came, but it came in God's time and in His way. I was just fortunate enough to be able to share in the moment.

In God's Time and In His Way

Had not those people already suffered for many days, weeks, months, or even years before I had the privilege of praying the prayer of faith over them? When they appeared before me, it was their season to reap the prayers they had long prayed for themselves, and I was just the instrument God chose to use to bring in the harvest. It was His time.

Many people have come into my meetings and are instantly filled with the Holy Spirit, but how

ALL THAT TIME, HER HEALING WAS ON THE WAY TO HER, BUT IT WOULD ARRIVE IN GOD'S TIME AND UNDER THE CIRCUMSTANCES HE PREDETERMINED!

long might they have been seeking this blessing before that divine moment? There's no telling. I was just privileged to be the one to lay hands on them in the timing of God.

A young woman was healed from multiple sclerosis in my meetings, but how many months or years had she already suffered the devastating effects of that disease before that moment of healing? How many times had she prayed or had others pray for her without any apparent results? All that time, her healing was on the way to her, but it would arrive in God's time and under the circumstances He predetermined. Until then, she had to walk out her faith, believing God for her miracle.

Because we have seen God do things quickly or instantly, we much prefer to think of Him as an instant God. This is largely due to the fact that our flesh likes things done instantly. There's nothing like instant gratification.

Our Age of Instant Results

This is an age of instant results. Our whole world is now instantly linked, and we get news from the other side of the world through satellites within seconds. We use instant messaging to communicate with friends. We are able to connect to Internet sites around the world in seconds. We've gone far beyond the instant coffee our parents found so compelling in their time. Everything has now been speeded up through modern technology, and the whole world moves at a much faster pace.

But although our world has changed, God hasn't changed. He is not bound by our expectations or our desires. He moves when He is ready to move. He releases a thing when He is ready to release it. When we pray, He will answer, but He will do it in His own time and in His own way. The blessing will come, but it will come in the moment God has set for it — and not before.

If we would have had our way, the entire Bible would have appeared instantly out of the fire of Mt. Moriah. Instead, God gave a little piece of His revelation in Genesis, another in Exodus, and a third in Deuteronomy, and so on until the whole volume was compiled. Does that make the Bible any less miraculous? Of course not. God's Word had to come to us in God's way.

In the Old Testament, we don't even find the name of Jesus. He appears there only in types and shadows of what was to come. It was only when the New Testament was revealed that the fullness

ALTHOUGH OUR
WORLD HAS CHANGED,
GOD HASN'T CHANGED.
HE IS NOT BOUND BY
OUR EXPECTATIONS OR
OUR DESIRES. HE MOVES
WHEN HE IS READY TO
MOVE!

of God's Word came to us. And God is still revealing Himself today in the same way.

We No Longer Needed Types and Shadows

After Jesus came, we no longer needed shadows and types. He was the real thing. We no longer needed bits and pieces of revelation about His coming. He is The Revelation. Suddenly that Revelation was in the world, walking and talking, performing miracles and changing lives. Although we are living in a very different time now, God has not changed. He still sets the pace and designates the day and hour of our specified answer. And you can be sure that in His time, it will arrive at your doorstep.

The fact that God chooses to work in this piecemeal way does not make what He does any less miraculous. And just because you're not seeing all that you want to see right this moment doesn't mean that it won't happen. It will, so get ready for it.

This is to be a book of faith and excitement for you. God wants you to know that even if you have not yet received your miracle or your blessing, it's on its way to you. Delay never means denial. God hears your prayers, and He will not withhold anything good from you. There is nothing stingy about our God. He is generous with all. So rejoice today, for your promises are on the way. The fulfillment of God's word to you is on the way. Your ministry is on the way. Your healing is on the way. Your blessing is on the way. *YOUR Camels Are Coming!*

CHAPTER 4

The Characters in this Divine Drama

Now Abraham was old, well advanced in years, and the Lord had blessed Abraham in all things. And Abraham said to the eldest servant of his house [Eliezer of Damascus], who ruled over all that he had, I beg of you, put your hand under my thigh; and you shall swear by the Lord, the God of heaven and earth, that you will not take a wife for my son from the daughters of the Canaanites, among whom I have settled. But you shall go to my country and to my relatives and take a wife for my son Isaac. Genesis 24:1-4

The story goes that Abraham assigned his most trusted servant the responsibility of finding a wife for his son Isaac. This servant, named Eliezer, ruled over Abraham's house and all that Abraham owned. Abraham told Eliezer to put his hand under his thigh and to swear by the Lord that he would not take, for his son Isaac, a wife from among the daughters of the Canaanites. Isaac's bride would have to come from Abraham's own country. This act of Eliezer, putting his hand under Abraham's thigh and swearing by the Lord, was a sign of agreement to perform all that his master required of him.

Many Valuable Types and Shadows

These scriptures speak to us of Abraham, Isaac, Eliezer and Rebekah, the beautiful bride found for Isaac, and their story also presents us with many valuable types. Abraham, for example, is a type of the Father, who is now sending forth Eliezer, a type of the Holy Spirit into the earth, to find Rebekah, a suitable bride for Isaac, a type of our Lord Jesus.

Taking on the Breath of God

The name *Abraham*, according to *Strong's* (#85), means *"father of a multitude."* Again, Abraham

ISAAC'S BRIDE WOULD HAVE TO COME FROM ABRAHAM'S OWN COUNTRY!

is a type of our heavenly Father, the Father of a multitude.

Abraham's name had originally been Abram, but then God made a covenant with him, and when a covenant was made, there was always a name change. In the same way, when there is a marriage, there is a covenant, and that is why there is a name change in which the bride takes on the family name of the groom.

In this covenant the Lord made with Abram, Abram was the bride and God was the groom, and so Abram's name took on a part of the name of God. When this happened, Abram was change to Abraham. The "am" sound of Abram's name changed to take on part of the name of God or, quite literally, the breath of God. Thus, the "ah" sound was added and Abram became Abr(ah) am, as the breath of God came into him. This was pronounced in Hebrew with the breathy sound, "ha."

This also spoke of the creative part of God. When He created the heavens and the earth, all was spoken into existence by His words issued on His breath. It was His breath, "ha," that would creatively bring into existence and bring about the fulfillment of all that God had spoken in covenant with Abraham.

The God of Abraham

When this covenant took place and Abram's name was changed to Abraham, God then became the God of Abraham. He had not been a personal God until the time that Abraham took His name through the covenant they made with one another. From then on, to all generations, He would be known as "the God of Abraham."

Later, of course, God became the God of Abraham, Isaac and Jacob, because the covenant that He had made with Abraham was to be extended to his seed and his seed's seed. Isaac and Jacob were the seed of Abr(ah)am.

Sarai Was Also Changed

In a similar way, Sarah's name had been Sarai, but she, too, experienced a name change. Because the covenant made with Abraham also included Sarai, her name also took on the breath of God. No longer would she be known as Sarai, ending in ai; her name now became Sar(ah). The covenant God made with Abraham also included his wife. It was to be through Sarah that Abraham's seed would come forth and bring about the fulfillment of the promises that came from the voice of God, upon His breath, "ah."

ISAAC IS A TYPE OF THE SON, JESUS CHRIST, WHO TOOK HIS RIGHTFUL PLACE AND IS NOW SEATED AT THE RIGHT HAND OF HIS FATHER, GOD ALMIGHTY!

Isaac

The name *Isaac* (*Strong's* #3327) means *"laughter or merriment,"* but his name also means *"to take the right-hand side of."* Isaac is a type of the Son, Jesus Christ, who took His rightful place and is now seated at the right hand of His Father, God Almighty. Jesus is our Lord and Savior and our soon-coming King.

Eliezer

The name *Eliezer* (*Strong's* #461) means *"God of help."* According to *Strong's* (#410), the first part of this name, *El*, means *"mighty, Almighty, deity, power"* (it is the name of God), and the second part of the name, *ezer* (*Strong's* #5828), means *"aid, help."* In other words, he is the one who looks out for and over us. Therefore, the full name means *"deity, mighty one, the one who aids, helper."* Thus, Eliezer is a type of the Holy Spirit, and the Holy Spirit is God. He is the Mighty One who makes us mighty with His power. It is the Holy Spirit who comes to our aid and is our Helper in every time of need.

Rebekah's name

The name *Rebekah (Strong's #7259)* means *"to clog by tying up the fetlock, fettering (by beauty)."* A *fetlock* is *"a projection bearing a tuft of hair on the back of the leg above the hoof of a horse or similar animal."* To *clog* means *"to add a weight to a man or an animal; to hinder motion; something that shackles or impedes movement."*

To clog the fetlock is *"to place a weight, or shackle, around the tuft of hair above a horse's hoof to hinder its movement."* Horses that drew carriages, after arriving at a particular destination, would be clogged by the driver. Weights would be placed around the fetlock to keep the horse stationary and to hinder any movement of the animal. To *fetter* is *"to restrain from motion or action."* Rebekah had such a beauty about her.

Rebekah as a Type of the Bride of Christ

Rebekah is a type of the Bride of Christ. When we become part of the Bride of Christ, our lives are no longer our own. We have been bought with a price. Because of the Lord's great love for us, He will, at times, clog us in order to keep us from moving (except when He wants us to move)

WHEN WE BECOME
PART OF THE BRIDE OF
CHRIST, OUR LIVES ARE
NO LONGER OUR OWN.
WE HAVE BEEN BOUGHT
WITH A PRICE!

but to keep us standing still when He wants us to wait for His leading and direction. He becomes the Director of our lives.

When we are married to the Lord, we are bound to Him with fetters of love. As we behold Him and we see His beauty and His magnificence, we are yoked to Him, fettered to Him, bound to Him, in love. When He beholds the beauty of His Bride, He is restrained in His actions toward us. He withholds His wrath, is slow to anger, and is also bound to us with those fetters of love.

Eliezer's Mission

Eliezer, the type of the Holy Spirit, was sent forth to find a wife for Isaac, a type of our Bridegroom, Jesus Christ. Isaac's bride could not be found among the Canaanites. In other words, the Bride of Christ cannot be of the world or of those who oppose the Kingdom of God. She must be part of His Kingdom. She must have His blood flowing through her veins. She must be related to Him.

So these are the human characters in this divine drama, and then there were the camels. They, too, had an important role to play. Let's get to those camels now, and remember: *YOUR Camels Are Coming!*

CHAPTER 5

The Journey

And the servant took ten of his master's camels and departed, taking some of all his master's treasures with him.   Genesis 24:10

Eliezer, as a representation of the Holy Spirit, willingly accepted his charge. He took with him ten camels, and this is significant because the number ten speaks of reward or judgment.

These camels were loaded down with his master's treasures. The King James Version of the Bible says, *"... for all the goods of his master were in his hand."* The New Living Translation renders this phrase as: *"taking with him the best of everything his*

master owned." This obviously speaks of the blessings and rewards of the Lord.

The ten camels were loaded down with the treasures of the kingdom — provision, blessings, and
gifts — and, in the same way, the treasures of our
Father's Kingdom are on their way to the Bride in
these days. Everything that we need in this hour
for ministry is being released by the Holy Spirit.

Do you need a fresh anointing? It's on the way!
Do you need the power of the Holy Spirit? It's on
the way! Do you need finances? They're on the
way! Oh, the camels are coming with everything
you need!

Prophetic Insight

In December of 1999, I was on my way to minis-
ter in a meeting in the New Orleans area. God had
been doing such amazing things in the meetings
I was holding that we were in great anticipation
of what He had in store for us next. We had prophetically stepped into the "new thing," not really
knowing or understanding what it all meant.
We just knew that the Lord was moving, and we
wanted all that He had for us.

When I arrived at the meeting with several dear
friends and intercessors, our hostess began to
exclaim, "The camels are coming! The camels are

WE HAD
PROPHETICALLY STEPPED
INTO THE "NEW THING,"
NOT REALLY KNOWING
OR UNDERSTANDING
WHAT IT ALL MEANT. WE
JUST KNEW THAT THE
LORD WAS MOVING, AND
WE WANTED ALL THAT HE
HAD FOR US!

coming! I don't know what it means. All I know is that the camels are coming!" I knew immediately that the Lord had spoken to her, and I knew that what the Lord had been showing me for months was real.

That night, through His Word, the Lord showed us that the camels that are coming are loaded down with all the goods from the Master's hands, and they are coming to bear gifts to His prospective Bride. I saw that these camels were not small, scrawny and weak animals. They were huge, powerful beasts of burden, massive in size.

And these huge camels were heavily loaded. In fact, they were overloaded with everything the true Church, Christ's prospective Bride, needs for her success in all that is about to transpire in the earth.

The Camels that Came to Jesus

I find it interesting that Jesus, after His birth, was visited by wisemen riding camels loaded down with precious gifts. Those camels had come a great distance and were carrying a precious cargo. Among the gifts they carried were gold, frankincense and myrrh.

The word *gold* (*Strong's* #5557) means *"(through the idea of the utility of the metal) gold; a golden article, as an ornament or coin, ... from the base of #5530,"* meaning *"to furnish what is needed; to graze [touch slightly], light upon, to employ or to act towards one in a given manner: entreat, use."* Just as that precious gold was brought to the Redeemer of the world by camels that were loaded down, gold has now come to us, as God's glory is being revealed in the earth.

The baby Jesus was God revealed in the flesh, the Christ, the Anointed One, in the form of an infant, and the gold brought to Him signified that He was fully *furnished* with all that was needed to accomplish His great mission on earth, the redemption of all mankind. He had the touch of Heaven upon Him, and He was *grazed* by the markings of His Father. He was *lit upon* and *employed*. His Father was acting toward Him with favor because He would now be used and directed by His hand.

I see the camels coming to God's people, and they are loaded down with many different things — not just gold. This signifies to me that God's Church is being fully *furnished* with all that is needed to accomplish the Great Commission left to us to bring in a great end-time harvest of souls. The Father has *grazed* us. We are marked by Him

IT ONLY TAKES THE
SLIGHTEST TOUCH
FROM GOD, AND WE ARE
TRANSFORMED INTO ALL
THAT HE HAS CALLED US
TO BE!

and for Him. It only takes the slightest touch from Him, and we are transformed into all that He has called us to be. He has *employed* us to be laborers in His great vineyard. He is acting toward us in His grace, mercy and favor. He is entreating us to be used in His Kingdom.

The word *myrrh* (*Strong's* #4666) means "*strengthened for,*" (*Strong's* #4753) "*an armament, a body of troops; army, soldier, man of war,*" and (*Strong's* #4754) "*to serve in a military campaign; to execute the apostolate, to contend with carnal inclinations: soldier, (go to) war.*"

This word *armament* means "*military equipment, a military force, means of protection or defense, armor, the process of being prepared for war.*" *Apostolate* means "*the office of an apostle.*" Therefore, to *execute the apostolate* is "*to execute the office of an apostle.*"

Jesus is the *Man of War*:

> *Who is the King of glory? The Lord strong and mighty, the Lord mighty in battle.*
> *Who is [He then] this King of glory? The Lord of hosts, He is the King of glory.*
> Psalm 24:8 and 10

Jesus is the Captain of the Hosts, the Chief Officer of the armies of Heaven. He is the Lord of the Battle. He is our Armor, our Defense. He is the One who establishes and executes the *apostolate*.

We are His *body of troops*, and we are becoming a great army that will move through the earth, bringing salvation, gathering in the harvest and flowing in signs and wonders, to demonstrate to the earth that there is a true and living God. We are soldiers enlisted in the greatest *military campaign*. We are God's military equipment, a great *military force*, and we are in the process of being prepared for war. There is coming a great execution of the apostolic in the earth.

The word *frankincense* (*Strong's* #3030) means *"incense tree, or incense itself."* In the Scriptures, *incense* always speaks of intercession or prayer. Jesus became our Great Intercessor, and He has imparted to us the power of prayer and intercession.

Those camels that came to Jesus when He was but an infant traveled long distances and crossed unfriendly and inhospitable territory to find Him, and all the while, they carried the treasures Mary and Joseph would need to care for the child while they were in exile in Egypt. That was the beginning of the first day. Now we are in the third day, and it is no different in this day. As the camels went to Jesus in the first day, they will be sent to

WE ARE GOD'S MILITARY
EQUIPMENT, A GREAT *MILITARY
FORCE*, AND WE ARE IN THE
PROCESS OF BEING PREPARED
FOR WAR!

you and me to fully equip us for the hour we are living in.

Loaded Down

The camels that came to visit the young child Jesus were loaded down with gold, frankincense and myrrh, and the camels are now coming again, bringing to the Lord's Church all that is needed for her equipping in this hour.

The gold dust or the sprinkling of other colors that is coming into our meetings is not an end in itself. It is God's visible, manifested glory, and when it is revealed, it is just a glimpse of many greater things to come. It is a symbol of God's power. He is preparing to do far greater things through His Body, His Church, His prospective Bride.

We have no way of knowing how long the journey took for Eliezer to reach his destination. What we do know is that he got there. We have no way of knowing what difficulties he may have faced along the way. The important thing is that nothing was allowed to hinder this important mission. Whatever he encountered and however long the journey took, Eliezer arrived in Mesopotamia to the city of Nahor. And I can say with certainty: *YOUR Camels Are Coming!*

The Events Leading Up

God tested and proved Abraham and said to him,
Abraham!
And he said, Here I am.
[God] said, Take now your son, your only son
Isaac, whom you love, and go to the region of
Moriah; and offer him there as a burnt offering
upon one of the mountains of which I will tell
you. Genesis 22:1-2

In the chapters leading up to Genesis 24, we can
see a plan developing for the coming of the camels.
Here in chapter 22, we see Abraham being required
by God to offer his son Isaac as a sacrifice. This is
a picture of the death and resurrection of the Lord

Jesus Christ, for Isaac was a type of the Christ who was to be offered up as a sacrifice by God the Father.

In the end, a ram was found stuck in the thicket. It was provided by God Himself to take Isaac's place. That ram was symbolic of the sacrifice of the Lamb of God, who has taken our place in death. We were the ones who deserved to die upon the altar of sacrifice, but God provided a Lamb to take our place. That Lamb is none other than the Lord Jesus Christ!

The Death of Sarah

In chapter 23, we find the death of Sarah:

> *Sarah lived 127 years; this was the length of the life of Sarah. And Sarah died in Kiriath-arba, that is, Hebron, in the land of Canaan. And Abraham went to mourn for Sarah and to weep for her.* Genesis 23:1-2

Sarah had been a type of the Bride of Christ. But now she had died, the old had passed away, and the new was coming on the scene.

Esther As a Third-Day Bride

In the powerful story of Esther, she was a third-

WE WERE THE ONES
WHO DESERVED TO DIE
UPON THE ALTAR OF
SACRIFICE, BUT GOD
PROVIDED A LAMB TO
TAKE OUR PLACE!

day bride, a type of you and me in the earth at this particular time in the eternal plans and workings of God the Father. Esther was appointed and anointed for a specific role and took a position much like that of Rebekah in Genesis 24.

Esther's story is complicated by the fact that there was a queen already in the land. Her name was Vashti. But Vashti displeased her king and had to be removed and replaced.

One day King Ahasuerus put on a great feast for all of his lords. At just the right moment, he called for his bride to come forth so that her beauty could be seen and appreciated by all, but something happened. Surprisingly, the queen refused the king's request, and this caused the king to be embarrassed, hurt and angry.

Picture the Scene

Picture the scene: The king had allowed the build-up of the activities until just the right moment, and then he was about to have a curtain pulled back so that his beautiful queen could be revealed. But, to his utter dismay, she had other ideas and left him in disappointment.

In the very same way, a curtain is about to be pulled back, and the Bride of Christ is about to be revealed to the whole world. Jesus wants very much to display His Bride in all the earth, but this requires our active participation. Whatever you do, don't disappoint your Bridegroom.

What Vashti Did

We know what Vashti did. She refused to heed her king's call to be displayed at the banquet. She had evidently become so overcome with pride that now she considered herself more important than the king himself, and her own wishes were suddenly elevated above his. That act sealed her fate. She had to be removed, and this was symbolic of the removal of Israel as the wife of God.

Now a new bride would be sought for Ahasuerus, and very soon a call went forth in the land for the most beautiful virgins in all the kingdom to come to the king's palace and begin to prepare themselves to tryout to see who would become his next queen. The current queen was out because she was not willing to come forth and be shown to the world. This, again, represented the setting aside of the Jewish people who had been destined to become the Bride of Christ. Her loss is our gain.

In the competition to find a new queen for King Ahasuerus, a young Jewish woman known as Esther, or Hadassah, won the king's heart and

REBEKAH HAD BEEN
DIVINELY RAISED UP
AS A THIRD-DAY BRIDE,
JUST LIKE YOU AND ME
TODAY!

became his new queen. She had been divinely raised up as a third-day bride, just like you and me today.

So in these chapters, we see the death and burial of Christ, His resurrection, and the temporary removal of Israel from the picture. And then we come to Chapter 24 and the selection of Isaac's bride. Abraham left nothing to chance. He sent his most trusted servant to accomplish this all-important mission.

In this way, Eliezer was sent to find a bride for Isaac, who, in a way, had just been raised from his (potential) deathbed. This also speaks to us of the calling out of the Bride of Christ. Herein lies the beginning of a new day, a new plan in effect for finding a bride for Isaac, a type of the Christ. This time it was to be Rebekah who would become the called-out-one, the one favored by God as a third-day bride, and the camels carried the treasures she would receive. Are you ready for *your* camels?

Abraham Was Highly Favored

Again, we see Abraham here as a type of our God, Father and King. The Scriptures state: *"the Lord had blessed Abraham in all things."* God Himself visited Abraham, and, turning toward him, revealed Himself to Abraham as El Shaddai, the self-revealing, fruitful God who has more than enough, the many-breasted God who could never be emptied of resources, provision, blessings or wealth. In other words, God revealed Himself to Abraham as the God who was about to bless him and his seed (which includes us) with all of the riches of the Kingdom!

It is believed that Abraham may have been the wealthiest man on the face of the earth, and you and I are to be blessed with all of the riches of God's Kingdom as well. We serve a great God! We know that He owns all the cattle on a thousand hills. He owns everything. For instance, all the gold and silver are His:

> *The silver is Mine and the gold is Mine, says the Lord of hosts.* Haggai 2:8

Our Father is very wealthy and has plenty of everything we have need of. He is about to send things your way that it hasn't occurred to you to ask Him for. You didn't know to ask, but He knows what you need, and your camels are coming, heavily laden with blessings.

Abraham was blessed and fruitful, and because the camels were coming from him, what they bore had to represent him well.

IT IS BELIEVED THAT
ABRAHAM MAY HAVE
BEEN THE WEALTHIEST
MAN ON THE FACE OF
THE EARTH, AND YOU
AND I ARE TO BE BLESSED
WITH ALL OF THE RICHES
OF GOD'S KINGDOM AS
WELL!

God's Care

Abraham's camels were in the Old Testament. Then we had those camels that came to Jesus when He was but an infant. But God's care for His people did not end with the first century. Camels are even now on their way to the Bride of Christ, wherever she is found in the earth. If you have been born again into the Kingdom of God and have sanctified yourself for His purposes, then you have positioned yourself to become part of His Bride. That's more exciting now than ever because we're in the end-times, the culmination of all things.

Jesus' Crowning

I can somehow imagine what took place when Jesus arrived back in Heaven. He had been sent on assignment to give His life as a ransom for fallen man, had been crucified and had risen from the dead. Now suddenly He was back, after completing His mission.

Now royal robes were placed upon Him, and He was crowned with many crowns. In that moment, I can somehow see Him already dancing with joy around the throne of God, and with great excitement, saying, "I can't wait to get My Bride. I am longing so to see her." But the counsels of Heaven knew that getting her would take time. She must be readied, equipped and made worthy for Him.

Because His Bride would hold such an important position, care must be given to be sure that she was the right person. She could not be from Canaan, and she could not be a mere concubine. She had to be the real thing, the legitimate Bride of Christ. Then, she must be dressed properly as befits the Bride of Christ.

As time went by, I can imagine that Jesus, seated at the Father's right hand, might have exclaimed, "I can't wait! I just can't wait! She's looking so good to me! She's so beautiful! Let's send her some more gifts of jewels and finery! Let's cover her with gold!" He loves His Bride, and His Bride must love Him too.

Eliezer's Legitimate Question

The bride also had to be willing, and this concerned Eliezer. He had a legitimate question for his master that day:

The servant said to him, But perhaps the woman will not be willing to come along after me to this

JESUS WILL NOT COME
BACK HERE AND LIVE
WITH US. WE HAVE TO GO
TO HIM!

country. Must I take your son to the country from which you came? Genesis 24:5

Abraham's answer was unequivocal and strong: *Abraham said to him, See to it that you do not take my son back there. The Lord, the God of heaven, Who took me from my father's house, from the land of my family and my birth, Who spoke to me and swore to me, saying, To your offspring I will give this land—He will send His angel before you, and you will take a wife from there for my son. And if the woman should not be willing to go along after you, then you will be clear from this oath; only you must not take my son back there.* Genesis 24:6-8

You can't get any more specific than that. Jesus will not come back here and live with us. We have to go to Him. The Bride must go to meet her Bridegroom in His country. He will not live again in ours. It is not worthy of Him.

Yes, Jesus will eventually return to this earth, but when He does it will be to rule. He will have fire in His eyes and will be mounted on a magnificent white steed and will carry a sword in His hand. That's another time and another purpose. For now, the Bride needs to rise to meet Him in His realm.

We are now on a journey of great preparation, and the hour is late. We have stepped into the eleventh hour, but at the midnight hour there will be a shout, and we will go out to meet Him. Will you be ready?

Eliezer was right. The woman had to be willing. Are you willing? God can't force us, and He won't force us. We have to be willing.

One bride was already set aside because she was found to be unworthy, and the curtain is about to be pulled back. Will you be found willing in that hour?

Ahasuerus removed Vashti, and she was replaced. God divorced His first bride, and now He is searching for a Bride who will be worthy of His love. Will you be part of that Bride?

Eliezer agreed to the deal Abraham proposed and swore the oath his master required. What does that mean? It means that it is a done deal. The Spirit is committed to the mission. Jesus will have Himself a Bride. Whether or not you and I have a part in that drama is up to us. Our Heavenly Bridegroom is willing ... if we are. How about you? If you are willing, *YOUR Camels Are Coming!*

<blockquote>CHAPTER 7</blockquote>

The Hour

And he made his camels to kneel down outside the city by a well of water at the time of the evening when women go out to draw water.

Genesis 24:11

See, I stand here by the well of water, and the daughters of the men of the city are coming to draw water.

Genesis 24:13

It was a very strategic time for Eliezer to arrive at the well. In the evening hours all of the young women of the area came to the well to draw water. Because of this, the young men also came with the intention of searching out a prospective bride.

Since this was also Eliezer's mission, he was in the right place at the right time. No surprise there!

As we have noted already, this is the mission of the Holy Spirit in this hour. He is at the wells of salvation, searching for a prospective Bride for Christ from among those who are drawing water from those wells. He is on time. Let us even now go out to draw water.

It Was Late

The hour was late, it was evening time, and the sun was setting. The day was quickly coming to an end, and darkness was fast approaching. As Eliezer noted, this was the time of day when the daughters of the men of the city would go out to the well to draw water for the family's needs. You and I, at this particular point in God's time frame, should be at the wells of salvation drawing water from a well that will never run dry!

The hour is late. It is evening time, and the sun is setting. The day is quickly coming to an end, and darkness is fast approaching. Are you in position to be chosen?

The Woman at the Well

Early in His ministry, Jesus met a woman we

YOU AND I, AT THIS
PARTICULAR POINT
IN GOD'S TIME FRAME,
SHOULD BE AT THE
WELLS OF SALVATION
DRAWING WATER FROM A
WELL THAT WILL NEVER
RUN DRY!

have come to call simply "the woman at the well" (see John 4). Jesus and His disciples had been in Jerusalem and had attended a great feast there. The disciples had wanted Him to rest, but He insisted that He had a divine appointment to attend to. They went on their way, and He went to the well known as Jacob's Well for a preestablished and foreordained meeting with a woman in need.

This was not just any woman. This woman was despised and rejected, but Jesus had a word for her. When she asked why He bothered to speak to her (when Jews did not speak to Samaritans, and He was obviously a rabbi), He replied:

If you had only known and had recognized God's gift and Who this is that is saying to you, Give Me a drink, you would have asked Him [instead] and He would have given you living water.

John 4:10

If she was willing, salvation was coming to this despised and rejected woman.

Jesus went on:

All who drink of this water will be thirsty again, but whoever takes a drink of the water that I will give him shall never, no never, be thirsty any more. But that water that I will give him shall become a spring of water welling up (flowing, bubbling) [continually] within him unto (into, for) eternal life.   John 4:13-14

If you are among those who are continually drawing water from the well of salvation, you are a candidate to become the Bride of Christ. Let us put in our jars and draw them up full of refreshing and life-giving water from the God of Israel.

Our Evening

Just as it was evening when Eliezer arrived at the well, we, too, find ourselves living in an hour that is late. The day is en far spent, and it is the evening of the ages. The sun is beginning to set upon us, the day is quickly coming to an end, and darkness, even gross darkness, is fast approaching.

Darkness is encroaching upon our borders, and there are not many more hours left in the day. At the eleventh hour, expect to experience the greatest outpouring of the Spirit the world has ever seen. We might call it the Eleventh-Hour Revival, and it will be the culmination of every revival that has ever hit the earth.

ALL OF THE POWER
AND GLORY OF PAST
REVIVALS WILL BE
CONTAINED IN THIS
FINAL ELEVENTH-HOUR
ANOINTING, AND WE
WILL EXPERIENCE THE
GREATEST VISITATION
OF GOD EVER!

Think of what God did in former days through people like Kathryn Kuhlman, and think of what He is doing through the multitude of people He is raising up in this hour. But the best is yet to come. All of the power and glory of past revivals will be contained in this final eleventh-hour anointing, and we will experience the greatest visitation of God ever.

As noted, in Eliezer's day, it had become a custom for the young men of the city to go out to the well and watch the promenade of young women, searching for their potential bride. It was the unmarried women who were sent out to draw water, so it was a veritable feast for the eyes of the young men. "Which one will be mine, Lord?" they were praying. This made it an even more appropriate place for Eliezer to look for a bride for Isaac. Get ready. Get in place. *YOUR Camels Are Coming!*

CHAPTER 8

The Test

And let it so be that the girl to whom I say, I pray you, let down your jar that I may drink, and she replies, Drink, and I will give your camels drink also — let her be the one whom You have selected and appointed and indicated for Your servant Isaac [to be a wife to him]; and by it I shall know that You have shown kindness and faithfulness to my master.   Genesis 24:14

Eliezer set some strict qualifications for the bride-to-be for Isaac, just as the Holy Spirit has certain things He looks for in those who are to make up the Bride of Christ. Not only was the bride of Isaac to be of the proper lineage, beautiful to behold and modest, but she would have to meet Eliezer's requirements in regard to watering his camels. It was not enough for her just to receive and welcome him; she would have to offer to water his camels as well.

As noted, the camels were important, for they bore the load of gifts, and Isaac's bride must recognize their importance. If she was to receive the gifts sent to her, she must value them. God's great gifts will be given only to those who value and appreciate them. Although every provision is being made for the Kingdom, provisions will be given only to those who welcome them, recognizing their worth. All of the goods from the Master's hands, all the treasures of His Kingdom — the very best He has — are being loosed to God's people, but we must be willing and eager to receive them.

How Would Rebekah Respond?

Eliezer prayed that day. He had devised a test to ensure that he was selecting the right woman, and he asked the Lord to help him. The question was: How would Rebekah respond to this test? There was a specific sign that Eliezer prayed for, so that he would know that God had rewarded his

GOD'S GREAT GIFTS WILL BE GIVEN ONLY TO THOSE WHO VALUE AND APPRECIATE THEM!

efforts. When the right woman came along, she would not be offended by his need for water. To the contrary, she would also volunteer to water all of his camels.

Going beyond is the test God is putting His people to these days. It's not enough just to do what we can get by with. We have to be willing to go the extra mile.

The other women who came to the well that day were not very anxious to give water to a stranger, let alone enough water for ten stinky animals. Just as camels can travel days without water, they are also notorious for the amount of water they can drink when it is available (from 30 to 50 gallons or more).

The hump found on a camel's back is not stiff with bone. It is made up of fatty tissue that holds water, and when a camel has gone a long time without food or drink, that hump shrinks, even at times falling to the side. So the camels before Rebekah now were pitiful looking creatures.

If you've ever been in a desert, you know what those creatures were facing. They were hot, tired, dusty and plenty irritable. This was not lost on Rebekah, who, no doubt, was accustomed to seeing camels and knew their reputation for being difficult and also cavernous when it came to filling them up. Amazingly, after giving water to the stranger, Rebekah cheerfully volunteered to water his ten camels as well.

God is placing some tests like this one before you and me, and what interests Him is to see how we react to His tests. He wants to see us going beyond the necessary, so He'll know that we are not just like everyone else. We're somehow different.

Your camels are coming, but when they arrive, they may not look very good at all. They may stink things up a bit and seem intractable. With their humps deflated and hanging over, dusty and dirty from the journey, they may not be appealing in any way. You may wonder how they could have been sent by God, but know that this is only a test. God is proving you, and when you begin to go the extra mile, accepting what God has sent to you, everything that is on the camels' backs will be opened and given to you.

Rebekah was a beautiful woman, but her beauty was more than just skin deep. She did what Eliezer had prayed the right woman would do, and thus she identified herself as the chosen one. How about you? Are you the answer to the prayer of the Holy Spirit?

SOMEHOW REBEKAH
STOOD OUT FROM ALL
THE REST, AND THE
IMPORTANT REASON
WAS THAT SHE HAD
PASSED THE TEST!

The Test

A Quick Answer

The answer to Eliezer's prayer came quickly:

Before he had finished speaking, behold, out came Rebekah, who was the daughter of Bethuel, the son of Milcah, who was the wife of Nahor the brother of Abraham, with her water jar on her shoulder. Genesis 24:15

Rebekah fulfilled not only the test Eliezer set, but also the test Abraham had set. She was family. Rebekah also had other qualifications:

And the girl was very beautiful and attractive, chaste and modest, and unmarried. Genesis 24:16

There were surely other attractive women there that day, some of them must have been chaste and modest, and all or most of them were also unmarried. But somehow Rebekah stood out from all the rest. The important reason was that she had passed the test:

And she went down to the well, filled her water jar, and came up. And the servant ran to meet her, and said, I pray you, let me drink a little water from your water jar. And she said, Drink, my lord; and she quickly let down her jar onto her hands and gave him a drink.

Genesis 24:16-18

Some might imagine that what Rebekah had was a huge water jar, but how could she have handled that? She was a young woman, after all. What she had in her hand, clearly, was a young-woman-sized jar. She would be expected to bring home enough water for the family for their evening meal and some for the night as well, and still she was willing to give water to a complete stranger, knowing that she would have to go down and get more.

"I Will Draw Water for Your Camels Also"

Some of the others who were at the well that day might have done this much, but what Rebekah did next clearly went above and beyond:

When she had given him a drink, she said, I will draw water for your camels also, until they finish drinking. So she quickly emptied her jar into the trough and ran again to the well and drew water for all his camels. Genesis 24:19-20

SHE WAS WILLING
TO GIVE WATER TO A
COMPLETE STRANGER,
KNOWING THAT SHE
WOULD HAVE TO GO
DOWN AND GET MORE!

Camels have two stomachs, and they can drink huge quantities of water. Ten camels can probably drink several hundred gallons of water at one time, when they have been traveling for some days without water.

None of the other girls at the well that day ran to Rebekah's aid. They wanted nothing to do with such smelly, willful and rebellious creatures. But Rebekah knew how to make the camels her friends. So, although these camels were obstinate, rebellious, ugly and stinky, Rebekah agreed to water them, and it was hard work that would take her some time to complete. As noted earlier, on average a camel can drink up to fifty gallons of water.

There is no way to know just how much water Rebekah's jar could hold at one time, but even if we do a conservative estimate, it was still a daunting task for one person, and she was a young woman. Sometimes we are called upon to do some unpleasant tasks in the church, but know that it is just a test of your willingness to serve with a good spirit. You will always be rewarded. When you do such things with a willing spirit, you are watering your camels. This watering process could not have been pleasant, but a blessing was coming.

The Test

Eliezer Only Observed

While Rebekah was going back and forth to the well, bringing water to the ten camels, Eliezer stood by in silence, observing it all:

The man stood gazing at her in silence, waiting to know if the Lord had made his trip prosperous.
Genesis 24:21

It wasn't enough that the woman had vowed to water the camels. She could have grown weary and quit at any moment. Many start well, but never finish, and there was no guarantee that this woman would be any different. But Rebekah *did* finish, and that provoked a new response from Eliezer. She had no way of knowing that her response to Eliezer (a type of the Holy Spirit) and her willingness to serve would soon release more than she could imagine, including her destiny. Much was coming to Rebekah, the prospective bride. Her life would never be the same again.

What about you? Will you pass the Lord's test? Will you willingly yield to the movings of the Holy Spirit upon your life? Be faithful, for *YOUR Camels Are Coming!*

CHAPTER 9

The Preliminary Gifts

And when the camels had finished drinking, the man took a gold earring or nose ring of half a shekel in weight, and for her hands two bracelets of ten shekels in weight in gold.

Genesis 24:22

Just one of the bracelets presented to Rebekah that day would have been valued at more than US $5,000 in today's markets, but when she had seen those camels coming, she could not have had any idea what was on their backs or that it would ultimately be hers. Those camels could have been carrying grain, or they could have been carrying blankets or some type of garments. How was she to know? The point is that she didn't know, and yet she was willing to accommodate them. She was willing to be obedient to the promptings of the Holy Spirit.

Rebekah passed the test , and now all that had been sent by Abraham, a type of our Father God, was about to be released to her. All the goods of the master's hands were on those camels' backs, and they had been sent for Isaac's bride.

When the watering was complete, it was then that the gifts carried by the camels began to be opened, and Rebekah received her reward. This is what's happening right now in the earth. We are in the third day, and the Spirit of God is dressing His third-day Bride. He is releasing the glory of Heaven upon her. He is presenting jewels to the prospective Bride.

It has been, for many centuries, a common practice among the Jewish people that a bridegroom should present jewels to his prospective bride. In this way, he marks her as his own, and Father God is doing the very same thing with us. He is marking us, clearly identifying us as His.

I have a photo of a Jewish Orthodox bride, and in the photo it is difficult to see the bride's garments because she is so covered with jewels. There are necklaces, bracelets, broaches and every other

WHEN THE WATERING
WAS COMPLETE, IT WAS
THEN THAT THE GIFTS
CARRIED BY THE CAMELS
BEGAN TO BE OPENED,
AND REBEKAH RECEIVED
HER REWARD!

imaginable type of jewelry. Just before the wedding is to take place, the bridegroom comes and smears golden dust over her face and hands, those parts not already covered with jewels.

The moment Eliezer took out those jewels and presented them to Rebekah any young man who was standing by watching her with interest suddenly knew that he no longer had a chance. This particular woman was not available to him. She was spoken for. "Hands off!" the jewelry said. "She's mine!"

This is the same custom we have today when a prospective bride puts on an engagement ring. This marks her as spoken for. She belongs to another, and it is hands off for all other men.

In these days, as the Lord pours out the wonders of Heaven upon us, the enemy has to stand back. We are marked for union with the King of Heaven, and no one else has any right to us. We have royal blood flowing through our veins, and the enemy must back off.

Welcoming the Camels

Again, let's return to the idea of seeing smelly camels approaching and yet welcoming them. This was phenomenal. With everything that God allows to come into our life, there is a purpose. For instance, there is always a purpose for the things that come against us and seem to want to do us harm. There is a purpose for the things of daily life that seem like drudgery. There is a purpose for the unpleasantness that sometimes surrounds us. Even when fear and doubt and unbelief assail you, God has a purpose. You are being tested. Stand fast, for your camels are coming. Learn to deal with whatever tries to assail you, and the result will be that God lavishes you with the treasures of Heaven.

Rebekah did not know that there were treasures on those camels' backs, but as soon as she passed the test, the treasures were opened to her. We, too, have to pass our tests.

As we were growing up, we used to see those snowy pictures on television that said, "This is a test." Well, every time the devil comes to tempt you, it's just a test. Every time a cashier makes a mistake and gives you more change than was due you, it's a test. You can pocket that money and consider that God is blessing you, or you can recognize it as a test and gain a greater reward by correcting her mistake.

Every time bad things begin to happen in your life, see that snowy screen before you with its all

YOU HAVE TO PASS THE TEST TO GAIN THE REWARD THAT AWAITS YOU!

important message: THIS IS A TEST. You have to pass the test to gain the reward that awaits you. Press forward without fear.

The moment you pass the test, the covering comes off of the treasures—the jewels, the finances, or the provision you so desperately need. They were right there on the backs of those camels all along. And today, *YOUR Camels Are Coming!*

CHAPTER 10

The Need to Make Room

And [Eliezer] said, Whose daughter are you? I pray you tell me: Is there room in your father's house for us to lodge there?   Genesis 24:23

Once Eliezer had placed the preliminary gifts upon Rebekah, he asked two important questions of her:

1. *Whose daughter are you?*
2. *Is there room in your father's house for us to lodge there?*

What did he mean by *"whose daughter are you?"* He meant: Are you part of the family? That was a

119

crucial question. When Abraham sent Eliezer on his mission, he was to be sure that Isaac's bride came from the same family, not from among the Canaanites or any other bloodline connected to the enemies of God. Today the blood of Christ must flow through His Bride.

This question was immediately followed by another, equally important, question: *"Is there room?"* Oh, what an important question! And this is what the Holy Spirit is asking you today. Can you make room for Him? Can you make room for what He wants to do?

Those who want power with God have to make room for it. For one thing, they have to make time for it. Many of us who are Spirit-filled know that the secret of gaining more power with God is to pray more in the Spirit, speaking in tongues. But the question is: do we have time for it? Most modern Christians don't, so they remain powerless.

If you want to be used by God in the gifts of the Spirit, spend more time praying in tongues. If you want to know God's will and understand His Word, then spend more time praying in tongues. If you want to more easily overcome temptations or you need a breakthrough in some area of your spirit life, spend more time praying in tongues. We all know how powerful this is, but

MANY OF US WHO ARE SPIRIT-FILLED KNOW THAT THE SECRET OF GAINING MORE POWER WITH GOD IS TO PRAY MORE IN THE SPIRIT, SPEAKING IN TONGUES. BUT THE QUESTION IS: DO WE HAVE TIME FOR IT?

most people today just don't have time (or won't make time) to do it. It is our heavenly language that goes before us when we know not how to pray or what to pray.

We have time for everything else. We make time for what's important to us. But is there room for God? Is there room for revival? Is there room for the moving of the Holy Spirit? Or have we crowded Him out by giving our time to everything else but Him? It's an important question, and only you can answer it.

The Right Questions and the Right Answers

Eliezer had the right questions, and Rebekah had the right answers:

> *And she said to him, I am the daughter of Bethuel son of Milcah and [her husband] Nahor. She said also to him, We have both straw and provender (fodder) enough, and also room in which to lodge.* Genesis 24:24-25

Not only was Rebekah of the right bloodline, and not only was she willing to host Eliezer; she was also prepared. There was provision for Eliezer's camels. This family had obviously made it a priority not to miss opportunities like this one, and this attitude would result in blessings for all of them.

What about you? Is there room for the Holy Spirit in your life? When a time of visitation from the Spirit comes, we must always make room for it.

The Whole Family Was Affected

Rebekah rushed home to prepare for their visitor, and Eliezer settled down by the well to wait. Not long afterward, Laban, the brother of Rebekah, having heard from his sister about the man at the well and having seen the expensive jewelry the man had given her, came running. He knew that the jewels given to Rebekah had marked her to become Isaac's bride, and he had a message from the whole family. They all welcomed this man:

> *He cried, Come in, you blessed of the Lord! ... For*
> *I have made the house ready and have prepared*
> *a place for the camels.*   Genesis 24:31

Laban and the rest of his family welcomed Eliezer (the Holy Spirit) and showed their welcome by making

WE MUST BE SO READY
AND WILLING FOR THE
SPIRIT TO COME THAT
WE RUN AFTER HIM AND
WELCOME THE THINGS
HE IS CURRENTLY DOING
IN THE EARTH!

room for him. They quickly prepared their house for this great visitation, making room for this great guest, cleaning things up in preparation for his coming.

We are now in a season of great preparation, and a part of that preparation is getting things cleaned up and in proper order so that when the Holy Spirit is ready for a great visitation, we can say, "Holy Spirit, come on in! We're ready for You!" There must be no hesitation on our part. We must be so ready and willing for the Spirit to come that we run after Him and welcome the things He is currently doing in the earth.

Not only did Laban make room for Eliezer; he also made room for Eliezer's camels. When we open our hearts to God's Spirit and decide to give Him priority in our lives, it blesses the entire family. Laban was inspired to feed the camels and the men who handled them:

> *So the man came into the house; and [Laban] ungirded his camels and gave straw and provender for the camels and water to bathe his feet and the feet of the men who were with him. A meal was set before him.* Genesis 24:32-33

I'm not sure how much a camel can eat (ten camels in this case), but whatever it took, Laban was ready for it. And, if there were ten camels, then there were probably ten camel drovers, men with big appetites, and yet a meal was prepared for them too. In all of this, Laban did not know that even more treasure was about to be opened, and it was for him and his family, as well as Rebekah. You just don't know what is about to be opened to you. It's hidden, but it will soon be revealed. Most of us can hardly imagine what God is about to do on our behalf, but it will be revealed before long.

Many times our capacity for God is much too small, so small that it leaves no room for the Holy Spirit to move as He desires. The Lord wants to give to us more than we can imagine, but too many of us have boxed Him in. Our concept of the Lord is much too small. He wants to bless us with greater anointing, more power and more of His gifts, but we must enlarge our capacity for Him so that we can receive all that He has for us. Get ready, for *YOUR Camels Are Coming!*

CHAPTER 11

The Mission and the Decision

A meal was set before him [Eliezer], but he said,
I will not eat until I have told of my errand.
And Laban said, Say on.   Genesis 24:33

Eliezer must have been hungry from his long journey, but he refused to eat before divulging his mission. It was too important. Most of us would never delay a good meal for any reason, but there are more important things, and we need to get our priorities straight.

In Sequence and in Detail

Now Eliezer began to tell his story, and he did not rush it or leave out any part. It was too important. He told it in sequence, and he told it in detail: how God had blessed Abraham, how God had given Abraham and Sarah, two elderly people who had passed childbearing age, a son whom they named Isaac, about the commission Eliezer had received from Abraham to seek a proper bride for Isaac, about his doubts that a woman would follow him, about his master's assurances that the Lord would send His Angel before him to prosper his way, about his arrival at the well, about his prayer with specific tests, about Rebekah's amazing response and about his [Eliezer's] thanksgiving to God. I have condensed it into a few paragraphs, but in the biblical account it occupies many verses (see Genesis 24:33-49).

The detail of what God is doing in your life is also important. Every event has a divine purpose. Respond well, and your destiny will soon appear.

The Decision

And now if you will deal kindly and truly with my master [showing faithfulness to him], tell me; and if not, tell me, that I may turn to the right or to the left. Genesis 24:49

THE DETAIL OF WHAT
GOD IS DOING IN YOUR
LIFE IS ALSO IMPORTANT.
EVERY EVENT HAS A
DIVINE PURPOSE!

Having taken so long to tell his story in such detail, Eliezer now paused and welcomed some response from Rebekah's family. Before he could eat, he not only had to deliver his soul, telling them the details of his mission; he also wanted an answer from them.

It all came down to this, and what would their answer be? Would they consider this story to be too farfetched and not worthy of a response? Would they consider allowing their daughter and sister to accompany this man, whom they had never seen before, much too risky? Eliezer's words must have hung in the air for a moment, as everyone anticipated the response it should receive.

If that response was positive, then Eliezer would open more treasures and proceed with his mission in their house. If not, he would quickly be on his way, seeking a bride in some other quarter.

What Would the Answer Be?

Fortunately, this family had the right answer:

Then Laban and Bethuel answered, The thing comes forth from the Lord; we cannot speak bad or good to you. Rebekah is before you; take her and go, and let her be the wife of your master's son, as the Lord has said.   Genesis 24:50-51

Consider the fact that they had just met this man, and yet here they were making a full and complete decision immediately, with no time taken to think it over, no time taken to pray about it, no time taken to consider the consequences.

But what was there to consider? They immediately recognized that God was in this thing, so there was nothing more to be said, nothing more to consider, nothing more to pray about. They were able to reach a quick decision. How about you. Get ready, for *YOUR Camels Are Coming!*

CHAPTER 12

The Additional Gifts

Rebekah is before you; take her and go, and let her be the wife of your master's son, as the Lord has said.
And when Abraham's servant heard their words, he bowed himself to the ground before the Lord. And the servant brought out jewels of silver, jewels of gold, and garments and gave them to Rebekah; he also gave precious things to her brother and her mother.   Genesis 24:51-53

Eliezer had not yet eaten. He had taken his time telling his story and then asked for their response, and now, when they agreed to his proposal, he again opened his treasure sacks. There were more gifts for

Rebekah and also gifts for her brother and mother. God's Spirit has some *"precious things"* in store for you, too, and He will open them and present them to you the moment you give the right answer to His queries.

What Transpired the Next Day

By the time all of this had been done, it was quite late, so after they had all eaten, they went to bed. But early the next morning, Eliezer was up and ready to begin his journey back home. Rebekah's parents and siblings, however, were understandably reluctant to see her leave so soon. They pleaded for time:

> *But [Rebekah's] brother and mother said, Let her stay with us a few days—at least ten; then she may go.* Genesis 24:55

To most of us, that would not have seemed to be an unreasonable request, but Eliezer saw it differently:

> *But the servant said to them, Do not hinder and delay me, seeing that the Lord has caused me to go prosperously on my way. Send me away, that I may go to my master.* Genesis 24:56

GOD'S SPIRIT HAS
SOME *"PRECIOUS THINGS"*
IN STORE FOR YOU, TOO,
AND HE WILL OPEN THEM
AND PRESENT THEM TO
YOU THE MOMENT YOU
GIVE THE RIGHT ANSWER
TO HIS QUERIES!

God has a plan that must be fulfilled, so His priorities must take precedence over our own, as unreasonable as that can sometimes seem. Eliezer was driven by a divine purpose, and he could not be delayed for any reason. He had been sent to find a bride for his master's son, and he had done that. Now he had to get her back to be joined to Isaac. Nothing must be allowed to hinder or further delay that purpose. The bridegroom had waited long enough for his bride. He was now expecting her, and he must not be disappointed.

These were eternal issues that could not be de-layed because of personal feelings. And when God's camels show up at your door, you need to take it very seriously. By sending them to you, He is doing something of eternal importance in your life, and it must not be delayed or hindered for personal issues.

Rebekah Had to Decide

Ultimately the matter rested with Rebekah:

> *And they said, We will call the girl and ask her [what is] her desire.*
> *So they called Rebekah and said to her, Will you go with this man?*
> *And she said, I will go.*   Genesis 24:57-58

Think about it. Had Rebekah been able to sleep that night? Had doubts and fears of the unknown assailed her spirit? This was a life-changing decision she was about to make. Would it not have been reasonable to ask for more time?

No! Even Rebekah didn't need more time. This was her destiny calling, and she would be carried to its fulfillment on the backs of those stinky camels. And she was ready.

"I will go," she said, as hard as it must have been to leave her home and family and all that was familiar to her. "How could she do that?" some wonder. There was just too much at stake to do otherwise. She could not answer anything else or consider further delay.

The Decision Was Made

So the fateful decision was made. Rebekah would marry a man she had never laid eyes on, and in order to marry him, she would travel to a strange and distant land. But she was ready for whatever lay ahead.

So it was done. Within a very short time, Rebekah was mounting one of those camels, having bid her family a hasty good-bye. They blessed her and gave her a nurse and some maids to attend to

REBEKAH, THE PROSPECTIVE BRIDE, WAS SUDDENLY RELEASED TO RETURN WITH ELIEZER TO BECOME THE BRIDE OF ISAAC, JUST AS ONE DAY WE WILL BE RELEASED SUDDENLY FROM THIS EARTH TO GO AND BE WITH OUR HEAVENLY BRIDEGROOM, JESUS!

her needs, and then they stood and waved good-bye as she disappeared beyond the horizon.

Rebekah was a very special lady, and her family would deeply feel the loss of her presence, but they all sensed that God had something better in mind for her and them. The magnificent gifts Eliezer had left behind served to soothe their wounded spirits that day and in the days to come. They were not losing Rebekah. She was leading them all into a much better life.

In this way, Rebekah, the prospective bride, was suddenly released to return with Eliezer to become the bride of Isaac, just as one day we will be released suddenly from this earth to go and be with our heavenly Bridegroom, Jesus. Eliezer, representing the Holy Spirit, had given the prospective bride more jewels of gold and silver as part of the finalizing of the betrothal. Wow! Get ready. I just know it: *YOUR Camels Are Coming!*

CHAPTER 13

The Ride to Destiny

And Rebekah and her maids arose and followed the man upon their camels. Thus the servant took Rebekah and went on his way. Genesis 24:61

Once Rebekah was on the camel and on her way, she, as well as her family, had more time to think about what had just happened. How quickly it had all transpired! What a quick work had been done! One day she was living her life in the normal way, and the next day she was on her way to a totally new life. How great is our God!

But what had been the key to it all? Being willing to water those smelly camels had been Rebekah's test, and when she had completed it, the treasures had begun to open to her.

Fortunately, her willingness had stretched far beyond watering the camels. She had welcomed the stranger into the family home, and now she was accompanying him back to his land. When God begins to do something in our lives, it doesn't take Him long.

Enjoying the Ride

Now Rebekah was rocking back and forth on top of one of those camels. How ironic that those smelly beasts had become her friends and were carrying her to her ultimate destiny. I'm sure they were no longer ugly to her. They were beautiful creatures, creatures of destiny, creatures of blessing. It's amazing how our outlook can change once we catch a glimpse of the eternal.

Those camels had a holy purpose. As smelly as they were, they were there for a reason. They had been sent by God Himself, and on their backs had been many wonderful treasures. No, these camels were no longer ugly. What glorious and magnificent creatures! In that moment, they must have seemed to Rebekah like the most majestic beasts on the face of the earth.

WHEN GOD BEGINS TO DO SOMETHING IN OUR LIVES, IT DOESN'T TAKE HIM LONG!

Crossing Inhospitable Territory

On her journey, Rebekah would cross hot and dry deserts, but as long as she remained on the back of one of those camels, she would be able to endure. They would carry her through. She was about to go places she'd never been before, but the camels would carry her there, so she had nothing to worry about. They were taking her places she could never have gone on her own.

You, too, are destined to go to new places and have new experiences, and if you will stick with the camels God sends into your life, they will carry you there.

Since camels were fairly common in those days, there is no reason to believe that Rebekah had never ridden one. Whatever the case, she and her maids now had to go with the flow and allow the camels to carry them safely to their final destination. What a ride that must have been!

What Treasures!

What treasure had those ten massive camels carried? Something of everything the master had to offer, the best of everything. That was a lot of goods, and it was now all Rebekah's.

The camels, which had seemed so ugly only the day before were now so beautiful, and another reason is that they were now in their element. They were now fulfilling their unique purpose. Many things don't look good in our lives, but when we can see them in the context of their purpose and what they do to get us to our destiny, they look very different. Oh, for eyes to see all things as God sees them!

When we become new creatures in Christ, we are so rough, so crude. We don't know how to talk right or walk right. We don't yet know that there is a proper way for Christians to dress. New Christians often don't have a very good appearance to us. But God sees them as what they can become, not as what they now are.

When the people of Israel came out of Egypt, they were a sorry sight, a motley crew, and yet God saw them as a mighty army that would possess the Promised Land. He spoke to them and let them know that if they would stick with Him through the wilderness, He would remake them into a royal nation, and when they marched into Canaan, they would look like a kingdom of priests. Eternal purpose had come, and it had been transforming.

The same is true with new Christians. It doesn't take God long to turn them around and

SUDDENLY, THOSE SAME BABES IN CHRIST ARE SPEAKING GOD'S WORD, PROPHESYING AND MINISTERING TO THOSE WHO ARE IN NEED!

make of them something praiseworthy. Suddenly, those same babes in Christ are speaking God's Word, prophesying and ministering to those who are in need. They are standing behind the pulpit with powerful testimonies and bringing others into the Kingdom. Of course they are no longer babes. Purpose, brought to them by the camels God has sent into their lives, has transformed them, and suddenly they are magnificent.

Flowing with the Camels

Rebekah was flowing with the camels and, in this way, crossing new territory and getting closer and closer to her destiny. That journey, however, could not have been pleasant. For one thing, it was through hot areas.

I don't know about you, but I don't like the heat. I was a missionary for six years in Mexico, and it seemed that all I did was sweat in that 118° heat. But, in spite of the heat, I loved every minute of it. There was purpose and destiny in it.

Now it was Rebekah's turn to face the heat, the dust, the monotony and the uncertainty of the journey. But one thing was sure. Each clumsy step of the camel that bore her brought her closer to her beloved. And that must have been very exciting.

Are you excited about being joined to your Beloved? Get ready, for *YOUR Camels Are Coming!*

CHAPTER 14

The Arrival

And he [Isaac] looked up and saw that, behold, the camels were coming. Genesis 24:63

There are two ways to look at Isaac's role in all of this — as a man and as the type of Christ.

Isaac, As a Man

As a man, Isaac was also excited. He had waited a very long time for his bride, and although he couldn't be sure just what day Eliezer would return with her, he knew that the day of fulfillment was coming steadily closer. This caused him to have a little bounce in his step and a little chuckle in his voice. He was spending more and more time in the fields with the Lord, pondering what was to come, and with each new day, his excitement only grew. Those who knew him well noticed that he was spending more time on his knees than ever before.

Then one day he must have sensed that the time was now upon him. He had felt it all day, from early morning. The hours had passed, seemingly endless, with nothing new on the horizon. That is ... until now. Now, suddenly, everything had changed. Something was happening.

It was evening, and the day would soon end, but it would not end in disappointment, as had happened on so many other days. Isaac could feel something new in the air, something different, and before he ever saw the camels, he somehow knew that they were approaching. When he looked, it was only for confirmation. He somehow knew that his hour had come.

How Many Times Had He Looked?

How many times had Isaac looked in the direction from which the camels must one day come, and there had been nothing? Dozens of times? Hundreds of times? We cannot know, and it

HOW MANY TIMES HAD
ISAAC LOOKED IN THE
DIRECTION FROM WHICH
THE CAMELS MUST ONE
DAY COME, AND THERE
HAD BEEN NOTHING?

doesn't matter. The sight of the camels wiped out every disappointment of the past. The camels were now coming, and that was all that mattered.

In the fields that day, I am convinced that Isaac had been meditating on the promises of God. It wasn't the first time he had done this, and it wouldn't be the last. But now the promises suddenly came into view. The camels were coming.

In reality, the camels had been coming for many days already, and perhaps that is what Isaac had been feeling in his spirit. He couldn't see them, but they were coming. He couldn't see them, but they would be there. It would take time, but the camels were definitely on their way.

Isaac's Intercession

Isaac was not only meditating on the promises of God that day; he was also interceding for their fulfillment. We can do that too. We can bind things that would delay and detour our destiny and loose the things that will facilitate it. Nothing must be allowed to keep our camels from coming.

Isaac's blessing determined your blessing too, so as he interceded for his own destiny that day, he was also interceding for you. That was your spiritual mother riding on that camel, and nothing could be allowed to delay or hinder her timely arrival.

The Joy of Anticipation

Everyone close to Isaac had noticed his unusually joyful attitude of late, but now, as the moment of fulfillment neared, his joy was turned to laughter. As he meditated on the good Word of God and interceded for its swift fulfillment, a sudden chuckle came to him, and he could not suppress it.

That chuckle grew with time, until Isaac was ultimately laughing with anticipation. By the time his eyes beheld the camels coming he could no longer contain himself. He was what we call "beside himself with joy." If you've never experienced it, you don't know what you're missing. There's nothing quite like the joy of the Lord.

As Isaac's joy increased, I believe it began to shake the very foundations of Hell itself. There is nothing quite so powerful as a laugh of assurance. Perhaps the laughter of his spirit even caused the camels to move a little faster.

Now, not only were they majestic ships of the desert, swaying back and forth and moving gracefully forward, but there was an intensity to their

GET READY, FOR *YOUR CAMELS ARE COMING.* AND THEY ARE LOADED DOWN WITH ALL THE MASTER'S GOODS!

movement. They must reach their destination before nightfall.

Right now in the Spirit I sense God's camels moving swiftly toward each of us. They are magnificent creatures in their purpose and determination to reach us in the appointed time. Get ready, for *YOUR Camels Are Coming*. And they are loaded down with all the master's goods.

He Had to Look

But Isaac had to look. He had to lift his eyes. He could have reasoned that he had looked many times already, only to be disappointed. Why look again? Surely this time it would be no different. And yet he sensed that it *would* be different, and so he looked.

And it *was* different. The camels were finally coming, and upon one of them, placed in a prominent position in the line, was his bride in all her glory.

Oh my gosh! The very camels God had sent to test Rebekah and then bless her were used to bring her to her beloved and to her eternal destiny. How good God is!

They Caught Sight of Each Other

When Isaac caught sight of Rebekah, we can only imagine what went through his mind. She was more beautiful even than he had imagined.

At about the same time, Rebekah saw him and immediately got down from her camel and covered herself with her veil:

> *And Rebekah lifted up her eyes, and when she saw Isaac, she lighted off the camel.*
>
> Genesis 24:64, KJV

"Who is that man?" she had asked Eliezer in an attempt to confirm what she was feeling. His answer had been simple: *"He is my master"* (Genesis 24:65).

Rebekah had known it already, and the knowledge of it had caused her to jump down from that camel and run into the arms of her waiting bridegroom. What a sight that must have been!

Isaac, as a Type of Christ

That's how Isaac reacted as a man awaiting his beloved, but we have been studying him as a type of Christ. Just as Isaac awaited his bride, our Lord

JUST AS ISAAC AWAITED HIS BRIDE, OUR LORD JESUS HAS BEEN WAITING PATIENTLY FOR THOUSANDS OF YEARS FOR US, BUT NOW THE WEDDING DAY IS UPON US!

Jesus has been waiting patiently for thousands of years for us, but now the wedding day is upon us. His camels are much larger than any known to man, and they are ready to carry us to His waiting arms.

Isaac had been in the field that day meditating and interceding, and our Lord Jesus has been patiently following our progress and interceding for us at every turn of the road. We are not out of His thoughts for a single moment, and He will not be satisfied until we are safely in His arms.

No Disappointment

There was to be no disappointment that day, for Isaac or for Rebekah. She had found her bridegroom, and he had found his bride. And our story will end well too. I've read the final pages of the book, and we win the battle and live forever with the Lover of our Souls.

The story of Isaac and Rebekah concludes on a wonderful note:

> *And Isaac brought her into his mother Sarah's tent, and he took Rebekah and she became his wife, and he loved her; thus Isaac was comforted after his mother's death.* Genesis 24:67

The Arrival

Each of us has a happy ending waiting for our story. Don't miss your opportunity. Don't despise your ugly camels. Get ready for them. They will carry you to destiny. I declare to you: *YOUR Camels Are Coming!*

CHAPTER 15

Set in Motion

Everything has been set in motion. The Father, the God of the Universe, has sent forth His servant, the Holy Spirit, into the earth, for it is now the time of seeking a Bride for Christ. The hour is late, the Third Day has come, and it is the closing of the ages. The long-awaited promise from God the Father to His Son Jesus is about to be fulfilled. The search for the Bride has officially begun.

The Holy Spirit, represented by Eliezer, could not go forth empty handed. He took with him those ten camels, heavily laden. Those camels carried treasures that we can only imagine, things that go far beyond our comprehension. Oh, my, the things that God wants to do for us today!

Let's look at it one more time in closing. The New International Version of the Bible states verse 10 this way:

Then the servant took ten of his master's camels and left, taking with him all kinds of good things from his master.

As noted earlier, the New Living Version says this:

He loaded ten of Abraham's camels with gifts and set out, taking with him the best of everything his master owned.

The blessings the camels carried were *"good"* because the source of them was good. They were the *"best"* because our God is the best. The gifts of Genesis 24 came from Abraham, a type of the Father, and they had to represent him well. I can assure you that what God has in store for you and me is not only *"good"*; it is *"the best."*

As a new wave of God's glory sweeps over us, within it will be all of the things we have need of in life. The camels are on their way to you even now.

At the close of the day – the close of the ages — as the sun begins to set, we will be joined with

I CAN ASSURE YOU THAT WHAT GOD HAS IN STORE FOR YOU AND ME IS NOT ONLY *"GOOD"*; IT IS *"THE BEST!"*

our heavenly Bridegroom, and our destiny as the Bride of Christ will be fulfilled. And we will be with Him for eternity.

While we are still here on this earth, however, God's ultimate plan for our lives and the fulfillment of our destiny will come to pass, the ministry He has planned for us from the foundation of the earth, as we become the Bride of Christ here upon the earth.

Rejoice, beloved, for *YOUR Camels Are Coming!*

Author Contact Page

You may contact Andy McDougal in any of
the following ways:

AndysMinistry@gmail.com

www.facebook.com/andrea.mcdougal.3
www.facebook.com/andymcdougalministries

Phone: 225-572-9844

Other Books by Andy McDougal

THE
GLORY
OF
GOD
REVEALED

The What, the Why and the How of the
Current Revival of Signs and Wonders

Andrea "Andy" McDougal

HIS WONDERS IN THE DEEP

GOD'S CALL TO THE SUPERNATURAL

Andrea "Andy" McDougal

The
ARROWS
of the
LORD

Andrea "Andy" McDougal

The Power of the Seed

Andrea "Andy" McDougal

A Southern Lady's Tea Journey

A Legacy

Andrea "Andy" McDougal